On the Farm

Cattle
Cows, Bulls, and Calves

Lorijo Metz

PowerKiDS
press
New York

To Chris and Amy and their little herd, Eli, Lao, and Tai

Published in 2011 by The Rosen Publishing Group, Inc.
29 East 21st Street, New York, NY 10010

First Edition

Editor: Amelie von Zumbusch
Book Design: Greg Tucker
Photo Researcher: Jessica Gerweck

Photo Credits: Cover, pp. 4, 5, 7, 8, 9, 13 (top), 13 (bottom), 14, 17, 18, Shutterstock.com; p. 6 Lester Lefkowitz/Getty Images; p. 10 Patrick O'Malley/Getty Images; p. 11 DEA/ G. Dagli Orti/De Agostini/ Getty Images; p. 12 Laurie Campbell/Getty Images; p. 15 B. Anthony Stewart/Getty Images; p. 16 © www. iStockphoto.com/eliandric; p. 19 Peter Dean/Getty Images; p. 20 Gentl & Hyers/Getty Images; p. 21 Ariel Skelley/Getty Images; p. 22 © www.iStockphoto.com/Cynthia Baldauf.

Library of Congress Cataloging-in-Publication Data

Metz, Lorijo.
  Cattle : cows, bulls, and calves / Lorijo Metz. — 1st ed.
     p. cm. — (On the farm)
  Includes index.
  ISBN 978-1-4488-0687-4 (library binding) — ISBN 978-1-4488-1335-3 (pbk.) —
ISBN 978-1-4488-1336-0 (6-pack)
  1. Cattle—Juvenile literature. 2. Cows—Juvenile literature. 3. Bulls—Juvenile literature. 4. Calves—Juvenile literature. I. Title. II. Series: Metz, Lorijo. On the farm.
  SF197.5.M48 2011
  636.2—dc22
                              2010000479

Manufactured in the United States of America

CPSIA Compliance Information: Batch #WS10PK: For Further Information contact Rosen Publishing, New York, New York at 1-800-237-9932

Contents

All Those Cows!

Have you ever passed cattle **grazing** in a field and thought, "Look at all those cows!" What you might not know is that only adult female cattle with calves are called cows. Young female cattle that are not yet mothers are known as heifers. Adult male cattle are called bulls. Baby cattle are called calves, whether they are males or females.

Cattle are large animals. Even calves, such as the one on the left, are big. Newborn calves often weigh around 100 pounds (45 kg).

These cattle are Camargue bulls. Camargue cattle are a breed of cattle that come from a part of southern France called the Camargue.

There are many kinds of cattle. In fact, there are almost 1,000 **breeds** of cattle in the world today. People raise cattle for many reasons. Many cattle are raised for their meat. Lots of cows are raised for their milk, too.

Cattle are often kept in pastures. A pasture is a grassy place that is set aside for farm animals to graze in.

Four-Part Stomachs and Two-Toed Feet

Cattle are **ruminants**. Ruminants have special stomachs with four parts to help them **digest** grass and other plants. Food is softened in the first two parts. Then, it is brought back up to be chewed some more. This softened food is called cud. After a lot more chewing, it is swallowed again. Then, the third and fourth parts of the stomach finish digesting it.

Grass is hard to digest. However, the four-part stomachs of cattle and other ruminants are set up to break down grass.

Cattle are part of a group known as even-toed ungulates. They have two toes on each foot.

Cattle are also **ungulates**. Ungulates are animals with hooves. Cattle are not the only farm animals that are both ruminants and ungulates. Sheep and goats are, too!

Breeds of Cattle

These cows are Ayrshire cattle. This breed of cattle first came from Scotland. All Ayrshire cattle are reddish brown and white.

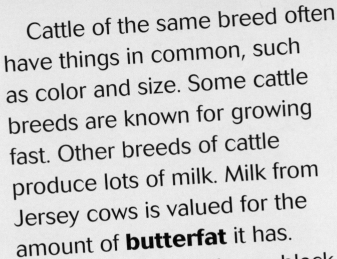

Cattle of the same breed often have things in common, such as color and size. Some cattle breeds are known for growing fast. Other breeds of cattle produce lots of milk. Milk from Jersey cows is valued for the amount of **butterfat** it has.

Dutch belted cattle are black with wide bands of white around their middles. You can likely guess how they got their name!

Farm Facts

Do you know how to tell one Holstein from another? Look at their spots. No two Holsteins have exactly the same pattern of spots.

Holstein cattle, such as this cow, are one of the most common breeds of cattle in the United States. Holsteins are either black and white or reddish brown and white.

American Dexter cattle are raised for their meat as well as their milk. They are one of the smallest breeds of beef cattle. This means they can be raised on small farms.

Cattle and People

In India, people have been raising cattle for thousands of years. Cattle are highly valued in India. Many Indians do not eat beef, but dairy products are important there.

Through the years, cattle have been important to people. Wild cattle were first hunted for their meat and hides. Cattle horns are hollow, so they were used for cups. In Asia, over 6,000 years ago, people began feeding and keeping cattle. This meant they no longer had to hunt as often.

Farm Facts

The first cattle in the United States were brought by Spanish settlers in the sixteenth century.

This ancient Egyptian carving shows a man milking a cow. The ancient Egyptians used cattle for both milk and meat.

In ancient Egypt, cattle were a sign of richness. They supplied food and clothing. They also pulled heavy **plows**. This made it possible for farmers to raise crops on more land. Goddesses who look like cows can be found in ancient Egyptian art.

Growing Calves

Cattle are **mammals**. Like human women, female cattle carry their young for nine months before they are born. After a calf is born, the first thing a mother cow does is to lick her newborn clean.

Highland cows, like this one, are known as good mothers. Highland calves are generally strong and healthy.

Shortly before her calf is born, a mother cow begins to make milk. An hour after they are born, most calves are already standing and drinking their mothers' milk.

These calves are twins. This means they were born to the same mother at the same time. Though cows sometimes have twins, they most often have just one calf at a time.

On some farms, calves drink their mothers' milk for several months. On other farms, calves are fed milk from a bottle. When they are about three months old, calves start grazing with the older cattle.

Cows like to stay close to their calves. Some cows have even broken down fences to find their calves.

13

Life in a Herd

Cattle are social animals. This means they live in groups. Groups of cattle are called herds.

When they are moving from place to place, the cattle in a herd often stay close together, as these animals are doing.

As people are, all cattle are different. Some are gentle, while others are nervous. Bulls tend to be forceful. Therefore, they are often kept away from cows.

In warm weather, cattle spend their days outside in the barnyard or grazing in the fields. At night and in cold weather, they stay in barns. Each day, cattle spend about 6 hours eating. They spend around 8

Some cattle herds, such as this one, have only a few dozen cattle. Other herds have thousands of animals.

hours chewing their cud. Cattle sleep only about 4 hours each day. While they may nap standing up, cattle lie down for longer periods of sleep.

What Do Cattle Eat?

Cattle are **herbivores**. Herbivores are animals that eat only plants. Cattle must eat up to eight times a day to get enough food. Depending on their size, they may eat as much as 40 to 100 pounds (18–45 kg) of food each day. Cattle also need water. They drink about a bathtub full of water every day.

This farmer is feeding hay to his cows. He is using a hayfork. Hayforks are big, long-handled tools used to lift and move hay.

Grass is the main natural food that cattle eat. Cattle that eat mainly grass are generally more healthy than cattle that eat mostly grains.

While cattle eat a lot of grass, they are also fed a mix of hay, corn, and cottonseed. Sometimes, cattle also get breakfast **cereal** and even potato chips! However, until they are three months old, calves drink only milk.

Dairy Cows

Some doctors suggest that kids drink a few glasses of milk each day. This is because milk has things kids need, such as calcium and protein, in it.

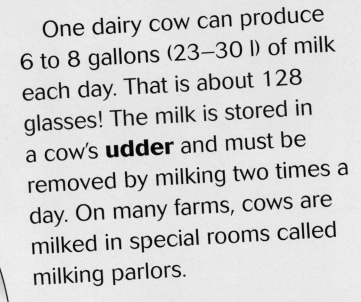

One dairy cow can produce 6 to 8 gallons (23–30 l) of milk each day. That is about 128 glasses! The milk is stored in a cow's **udder** and must be removed by milking two times a day. On many farms, cows are milked in special rooms called milking parlors.

Farm Facts

California, Wisconsin, and New York are the top milk-producing states in the United States.

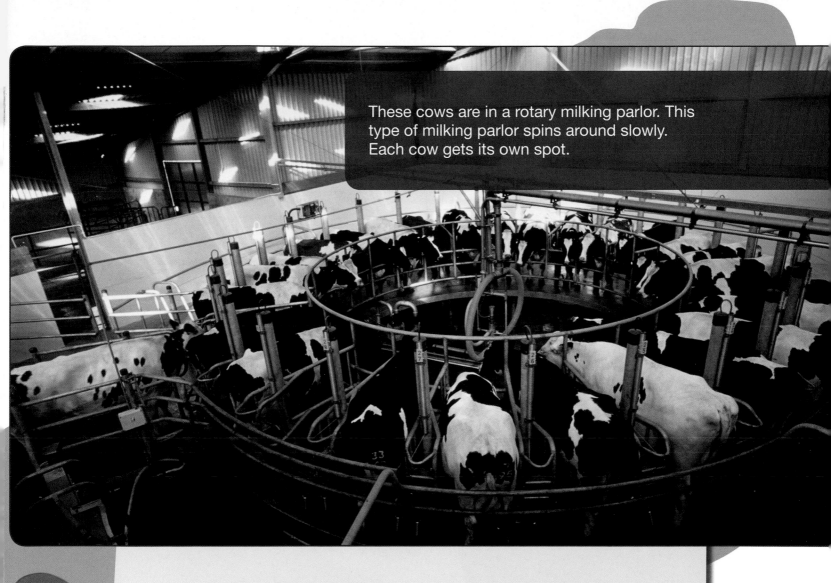

These cows are in a rotary milking parlor. This type of milking parlor spins around slowly. Each cow gets its own spot.

Many foods we eat, such as cheese, ice cream, and butter, are made from milk. Holstein cows are valued for the amount of milk they make. In the United States, they produce most of the milk we drink. Other common dairy breeds are brown Swiss, Jersey, and Guernsey cows.

Beef Cattle

These cattle are on a ranch in Wyoming. People have raised beef cattle in Wyoming for over 100 years.

Cattle raised for meat are called beef cattle. Most beef cattle are **bred** and raised on huge farms called ranches. There are many cattle ranches in the western United States. Texas is the American state with the most beef cattle.

Both bulls and cows are used for beef. Many foods you may eat every day, such as hot dogs,

Farm Facts

A cow that weighs 1,000 pounds (454 kg) can produce 432 pounds (196 kg) of meat.

This girl is eating a hamburger in a restaurant. Do you like hamburgers?

hamburgers, and steaks, come from beef cattle. Angus cattle are one of the top breeds of beef cattle in the United States. These cattle were first bred in Scotland. They can be black or red.

Beyond Dairy and Meat

You might be surprised by how many **products** come from cattle. For example, leather is often made from cattle skin. It is used to make clothing, such as coats, belts, and shoes. Some footballs and basketballs are made from leather, too.

This herd of cattle is in Montana. There are more than 2.5 million cattle in Montana. The whole United States has more than 90 million cattle, while Canada has more than 12 million.

Beef fat is used to make soap, crayons, paint, and even gum. Many paintbrushes are made using cattle hair. **Gelatin** made from cattle skin and bones may be used to make marshmallows and Jell-O. What would we do without cattle?

Glossary

bred (BRED) To have brought a male and a female animal together so they will have babies.

breeds (BREEDZ) Groups of animals that look alike and have the same relatives.

butterfat (BUH-ter-fat) The fat in milk.

cereal (SIR-ee-ul) Food made from grain.

digest (dy-JEST) To break down food so that the body can use it.

gelatin (JEH-lul-tun) Jellylike matter made from animal parts that is used to make certain foods.

grazing (GRAYZ-ing) Feeding on grass.

herbivores (ER-buh-vorz) Animals that eat plants.

mammals (MA-mulz) Warm-blooded animals that have a backbone and hair, breathe air, and feed milk to their young.

plows (PLOWZ) Machines used to cut, lift, and turn over soil.

products (PRAH-dukts) Things that are produced.

ruminants (ROO-muh-nunts) Animals that have stomachs with four parts.

udder (UH-der) The body part that holds milk in some animals.

ungulates (UNG-gyuh-luts) Certain animals with hooves.

Web Sites

Due to the changing nature of Internet links, PowerKids Press has developed an online list of Web sites related to the subject of this book. This site is updated regularly. Please use this link to access the list:

www.powerkidslinks.com/otf/cattle/